Don't Take it Personally

Blaming the Real Enemy, the Devil

IRWIN BROWN

ISBN
978-1-956529-99-9 (Paperback)
978-1-956529-98-2 (eBook)

Table of Contents

"Don't take it personally" was written with the hope of revealing a look into the "realm of the spiritual". A great deal of the negative events in our lives are designed to distract us from a "bigger picture". It is normal to believe that certain attacks are personal especially when the so-called antagonist(s) is directing an "assault" directly at us with the exclusion of other people around us. The enemy, the devil, *wants* to sow seeds of discord among God's people. He counts on it and is always around when strife is in the atmosphere. God wants us to look through the wiles of the devil and see goodness in each other, even our enemies.

If we could see that the devil was a major instigator in God's creation, there would a lot less strife among each other and the Earth in general. Unfortunately, the devil has a powerful influence and knows he can bring havoc due to our sin nature. If we would realize that the people that come against us are vessels that the devil uses, we would see that taking things personally is a detriment not only to us but to the individual(s) the enemy uses.

God requires that we see the goodness in each other even though some people choose to show us a side to them that is a detriment to God's mandate. Some people are empowered by strife and hatred. They are proud of the fact that they "agitate, instigate and manipulate", (AIMs) They are empowered by hatred; not understanding that they weaken themselves spiritually when they are on the attack. In the name of Jesus we are to forgive them. We are not to excuse he behavior but we should think of the words Jesus spoke "Father, forgive them, for they don't know what they are doing" Luke, 23:24, NIV.

The devil, the instigator

Persecution in any form can test the best of anyone regardless of how patient they are. It can also cause the person being persecuted to leave the "sphere" (or area of authority he has been assigned to by God) he is in during his "test". If you have been in an area where Satan has had an influence, your spirit or "light" will not leave his territory in the same shape it was prior to your arrival. While the devil's vessels may come against you while you are there, your presence will be felt after you are gone. In fact, prior to your arrival into an area that needed God's light, the enemy was already raging. Upon your arrival, the demonic influences increased due to the fact that demonic activity is stirred by the "light of God". Demonic activity increases because it is trying to negate the presence of the Holy Spirit.

An effort will be made to negate the presence of a godly vessel. Dark spirits, using people that do not know God, will come against you. These demonic influences are attempting to resist God's influences and will fight to stay "in power". It is a major reason why someone who is a vessel for God will find that they are the target of increasing persecution. If you are discerning demonic activity as persecution, you know you are being persecuted for God and you will stand strong in faith knowing that God will not forsake you. "The Lord himself goes before you and will be with you; he will never leave you nor forsake you. Do not be afraid, do not be discouraged", Deuteronomy, 31:8, NIV. The battle is spiritual, not physical. In the name of the "enemy", his vessels will attempt to drive you away from his territory.

Where ever you go, you may encounter opposition if you belong to God because the devil will stalk you in the spirit. He will attempt to harass and badger you. A person that the devil uses as a vessel may come against you in the work place and may recruit other people to come against you also. There is more times than not a "ring leader". This may be a superior in the work place or someone in your family or circle of friends. If so, these people are not to be feared because for starters, they do not know what drives them. They do not know who (or what) seduces them into thinking that you are their enemy. It is important to realize that so many have to bond in order to come against you. The truth is that they do not stand a chance with God on your side regardless of how many are against you.

Should you choose to leave an area where the devil has a strong hold, there will be a void or vacuum in that area because of the Holy Spirit's influence you possess. Conversely, when a mocker leaves, peace is restored because he too has had an influence; "Drive out the mocker, and out goes strife; quarrels and insults are ended', Proverbs, 22:10, NIV. The devil always likes to have agitators, instigators and manipulators (AIMs) at his behest. He will give his vessels authority over territory much like the Lord gives territory to His vessels.

The devil will tempt those he feels he can use into doing his bidding. Satan tempted Jesus with all the kingdoms of the world if Jesus would serve him instead of His Father, God, (Matthew, 4:1-11). This may have also been *another attempt* to take over God's kingdom as Lucifer attempted to take over heaven from God. Jesus stated in Luke 10:18, that "I saw Satan fall like lightning from heaven", NIV. If Jesus was tempted, *we* will be tempted.

Notice that in some areas, there seems to be more of the devil's influence than the Lord's. This is because the enemy can grant his vessel(s) authority over those areas. The people or person involved need not be in *positional* authority. In other words, they do not need to be a supervisor, manager, or CEO. They need not be a pastor, counselor or choir director. In fact, the enemy often uses people that are not in any *positional power* structure. He will use people that will appear to seem like the "least likely" as God does.

Stated earlier was the fact that if you leave an area that God assigned you to in order to bring about His presence, there will be a void or vacuum after your departure. Jesus' true power ensued after He was crucified. People you know will feel your "spiritual presence" when you are gone more than your physical presence when you were among them. If a couple of co-workers "have words" and someone insults the other, someone may say, "Julie would have *never* said that to anyone". In another scenario, a person you work with needs help. No one has time to assist. The person needing help may say. "Mike would have helped me, he was *always helping someone.*" People will miss your aura of peace. It may have *appeared* in your presence it was taken for granted. Some people appreciate what you bring to their lives.

There are times when an employee can manipulate a superior. When this occurs, the work-relationship changes and is now one of friendship instead of supervisor / employee. This was done because the employee *has taken the time* to manipulate the superior. Notice all the times the employee stopped by the supervisor's office to "chat". The employee used one of the devil's AIM's, (manipulation). In this particular case, the employee was a manipulator. His "aim" was to "get in good" with a superior. Now that he is in the good graces with the supervisor, manager or team leader, the employee can now "work" his manipulations.

The second method the devil uses is that the employee that has manipulated the superior(s) has found that there are people in the organization that have similar traits, (kindred spirits) with any adverse spirits he possesses (or at least they are gullible to his wiles).The term "kindred spirits" is used here but the employee does not know that because *he is not spiritually discerning,* "The person without the Spirit does not accept things that come from the Spirit of God but considers them foolishness, and cannot understand them because they are discerned only through Spirit", 1 Corinthians 2:14, NIV. The vessel's actions are demonically induced. The only way the employee can recruit other people at the behest of the devil is they have to have an avenue in which the enemy can work from anyway. If they did not have spirits of strife, conflict, anger, or envy, he could never infiltrate their hearts in the first place.

It does not matter who comes against you or how many. No one can come against you and defeat you. The devil gives his vessels the same "pride" he had prior to his eviction from heaven. His vessels think they should "take over" any realm they are placed in much like Lucifer thought he was entitled to take God's place in the universe. It is this pride that an employee and his cohorts have *in conjunction* with the given authority over a territory by the devil that drives them to create havoc and disorder. It will be noted here that a person with positon in a company often times will "cede" his or her authority to someone who is "gifted" in manipulation. If so, they have compromised their position. Any demonic spiritual influence *reverses* order.

When demonic influences are at work, order is reversed. People who are experiencing persecution often feel as if they are the least in any given realm where there are people gathered in that realm or territory. An example in a family unit is a child can feel as if he is insignificant. Someone at work with years of seniority can be made to feel as if they are one of the last hired, reducing their significance as a spirit, person and employee; *a by-product of persecution*. In the demonic realm, first is last and good is bad. Spiritual authority is also reversed; as person(s) who live for God will often be demoted, while people with adverse spirits, will be "exalted".

The Lord's presence will not be denied in any situation. Just as the enemy gives his vessels spiritual authority and territory, the Lord gives his vessels *His* authority and territory. The dark can never overcome the Light of the Lord. Ceding authority and territory to a satanic vessel is akin to giving the authority and territory to the devil himself. In the context of the work place, anyone bidding for the devil is looking for you to acknowledge them; *literally*, much like Nebuchadnezzar demanded that Meshach, Shadrach and Abednego worship idols or images of gold, Daniel 3:16-18, NIV. The term "acknowledge" is not to be confused with the respect a co-worker or superior is due because of decent work relations which is expected by the Lord.

The "acknowledgement" is used here to denote that a co-worker or superior requires that you worship them. As if you are not there for the company but for the authority they have over you personally. Your obligation to the company is of little importance to them. It is the same "pride" Lucifer possessed that got him kicked out of Heaven. Like Lucifer who had dark angels telling him how great he was, the people who want to "lord" themselves over you have been told similar lies. The devil gives his vessels *his* traits when he uses them. These traits of course will be detrimental to the vessels. Yet, to them (and their followers of their "inner circle"), these traits will be seen as attributes. *This is the way of the world.*

"When Haman saw that Mordecai would not kneel down or pay him honor, he was enraged", Esther 3:5, NIV. Mordecai would not bow to Haman because Mordecai would only worship God. "All the royal officials at the king's gate knelt down and paid honor to Haman, for the king had commanded this concerning him. But Mordecai would not kneel down or pay him honor", Esther3:2, NIV. When Mordecai still refused, Haman schemed to have Mordecai hanged and his people, the Jews, slaughtered, Esther 3:6. There are people you know that want you to kneel down and pay honor to them. These days the term is called "putting someone on a pedestal". If you do not put someone of this type on a pedestal, you will incur their wrath.

You will be targeted for spiritual if not physical elimination. The term spiritual elimination denotes an attempt to steal or rob you of your spiritual identity. The term physical elimination denotes, in the context of a job for example, that some people will plot to have you fired simply because you are not "buying" into their self-imposed superior selves. The "enemy" nor his vessels cannot have you in their midst without conforming. You are dangerous spiritually and professionally. Satan does not want the least amount of the Lord's kingdom in a domain where he thinks he has a foothold on. You are a threat *professionally* to the enemy's vessel because in many cases, someone who has God's light has the potential for positional promotion within a company although they already possess *spiritual* authority in the same domain.

People are God's greatest asset. They are valuable in His plans and obviously to His kingdom. They are vessels that He can use anywhere or time. There is a problem when wayward employees are not available to the Lord. They are "unprotected" and are vulnerable to the enemy's recruitment. When it occurs, havoc ensues. The devil is always looking for (and finding) people that will do his bidding. A hard-hearted person is a perfect candidate for the devil's recruitment. Some people think they can be hard-hearted toward people and be opened hearted toward God.

Since God is the creator of people, if you are hard-hearted toward people or anyone in particular, you become hard-hearted toward God because the two cannot be separated; people and the Lord of the Universe are connected. If you hate someone's relative, you, in essence, hate his family because he is connected to that family. Unfortunately, too many people *believe hatred is empowering.* They feel in control when they despise someone or a group of people and can even justify the hatred. The excuses used to hate someone will not suffice. More times than not, hatred is rooted in envy or insecurity. In the context of the work place or anywhere else, the *favor* the envied person appears to have is *spiritual,* not physical. His or her *position is spiritual,* not physical. There is a good chance that the person(s) doing the envying are confusing the concepts and do not understand that the same favor and positions in God are available to them. 'Then Peter began to speak', "I now realize how true it is that God does not show favoritism", Acts 10:34, NIV.

God has a strategic time to act on your behalf. There is a reason He may not act at a time we may want him to act. He may be in the process to see if any enemies will repent. He may delay moving on your behalf to build your faith. Understand that He made your enemies as hard-hearted as He hardened the heart of Pharaoh so the Israelites could witness the miracle at the Red Sea.

"But the Lord hardened Pharaoh's heart and he would not listen to Moses and Aaron, just as the Lord had said to Moses", Exodus 9:12, NIV. God *allowed* the enemy to manifest against you in order to grow and know Him.

Whatever your reasons, if you attempt to act on your own behalf, you will delay His plans to act. When He does act, God will "take care" of all enemies. The Bible states that *all ten* of Haman's sons were killed after Haman was hung, Esther 9:7-9, NIV. The snares your enemies set for you will backfire. *Haman was hung on the same gallows he had built for Mordecai,* Esther 7:10, NIV.

"Persecution" is not in your enemy's vocabulary. They are not aware when God acts on your behalf. Once they are humbled by God, the devil leaves them on their own, leaving them bewildered and wondering what happened. This is one of the devil's tactics; he uses his vessels and leaves them to deal with the aftermath of their actions. It does not matter what your enemies think or do; remember that their puppet master, the devil, while diabolically clever, is also the master of the "simpleton complex". He can use anyone but the people that are spiritually inept and not aware of his ability to use them are his best tools. These people, your enemies, are in bondage.

Are you a
free Spirit?

A free spirited person is someone that is a non-conformist; that is, they usually do not fall into any categories that would identity them. No cliques, circles and no "following the crowds". Normally, these types of people *tend* to be loners but are often very sociable. In the context of the job atmosphere, these types of people are the ones who typically state "I just want to come to work, do what I'm supposed to do and go home" The problem is that, that is not what some people want from you. They want conformity. They will create atmospheres that are conducive to strife. If you do not participate, the enemy will ensure his vessels vex you spiritually. A "free spirit" is not someone who does anything he or she wants to do. A "free spirited" is someone who walks with the Lord. *Jesus was free spirited in the context of what the Father required him to do.*

Free spirits can be intimidating to some people because they do not need other people to validate them. They can stand alone when necessary. Many people want you to "belong"; *to them* and do not want you to think "outside the box" nor be adventurous or step out on faith. Conforming to the will of what everyone else wants is the order of the day. *Being a free spirit in the context of the Lord is adventurous.* The Lord gave us the spirits of adventure and exploring. We are not here to live within the confines of people.

Respect

Anything God places within your heart is Spiritual. The Fruits of the Spirits of love, joy, peace, forbearance, kindness, goodness, faithfulness, gentleness and self-control are all spiritual in nature. Any ability or gift from the Lord is spiritual. Some concepts such as respect are also spiritual because it comes from the Lord and is placed within our hearts where it manifests itself as *self*-respect. Too many times we search for things outwardly that are readily found within us. One reason is because we confuse spiritual concepts with carnal concepts. "Respect" is not a carnal idea. It is a spiritual connection to God. *Self*-respect is the healthy regard for our individual selves that the Lord wants us to have in *Him*.

We look to other people to validate something that God has already validated. Whatever God has placed in your heart is not to be found in other people. If anything, many people may want to steal what God has placed in you. This is the dilemma for such people; they want to possess what God has placed in your heart on one hand and on the other hand, they want to *invalidate* the qualities God has placed within you. People are not to be looked to for anything God can provide. "Big me, little you" is the mantra that many people live by today. Discern that people who live by that mantra are projecting their insecurities onto other people.

There are people who do not know themselves in God. Whether you are a man or woman, God has given everything you need. There is never a need to seek "respect" or esteem from another human being. It is called *self*-esteem for a reason. It is the healthy self-love that has its' validation and authority from the Lord. Respect is not an intangible concept. It is not an exterior source. It does not have anything to do with economic status. It has nothing to do with social status. Many people look everywhere to find who they are. The answer is in the Lord. We often see the world in finite terms. Some of us identify the world and people in general in correlation to the way we view ourselves. We tend to think and see the world according to what is in our hearts. If there is a lack of *self*-respect, there is a tendency to think people around us do not respect us either because we believe people think the way we do.

Every day the Lord tells us how He feels about us. Every day He lifts and esteems us. He honors all He has created. How could anyone God has made in His image not be worthy of respect? "God saw all that he had made and it was very good", Genesis, 1:31. There is never a need to fight for respect; it is within you. The world teaches that respect must be fought for, literally. The prisons and graveyards are full of people, particularly men, who felt they were disrespected, and felt like they had to fight for it. *There are times when people can be disrespectful.* They are "full" of disrespect and their actions of disrespect have more to do with a void within themselves and have nothing to do with you. It is the way they operate; it is who they are. If someone does not have any self-respect, there will not be respect for you or anyone else.

Sometimes people who are disrespectful have to be "dealt with". There is a way to do so without creating a life-long catastrophe. The only path to self-respect is the narrow path God places you on, (But small is the gate and narrow the road that leads to life, and only a few find it) Matthew 7:14, NIV.

Who are you?

Who are you, *really*? What kind of people do you know? What is it that keeps you friends with them? The people you keep company with say a lot about you. It is very important that you monitor who you refer to as your "friends". Many people will be your friend with "conditions"; as long as you are providing them with what they need, you will remain in their lives because they have a use for you. You also have friends that want you in their life unconditionally; no strings attached. They may be better people for having you in their lives. You enhance them in some form without any thing *tangible* or physical. In fact they *feel* as if they are better people for knowing you. "He who walks with the wise grow wise, but a companion of fools suffers harm", Proverbs, 13:20, NIV.

In general, people tend to gravitate toward other people that they feel a bond with. Or, another way to state it is "kindred" spirits "locate" each other and bond. People are not always kindred spirits. Some people who are friends are not kindred but may have other avenues of compatibility. The very essence in any relationship is to enhance the well-being of other people whether in an intimate relationship or friendship in the traditional sense. It will be noted here that the emphasis is on *enhancing the well-being* (not harming) and bringing goodness to other people. There is a difference between "enhancing the well-being" of someone and *making someone happy.*

It is not up to you to make anyone happy nor is it up to someone to make *you* happy. If you are bringing goodness to someone's life and they become happy, fine. The problem comes if and when you are no longer available or cease to do whatever it is you were doing to make that person happy. Enhancement of someone's life comes when the person you are relating to is at least somewhat happy *prior* to your arrival in their life and they find that you have *added* to their well-being. This is not to say that people should be happy at all times. We know how unrealistic the idea is because life brings about tests and trials. The issue here is that "making someone happy" is an unrealistic burden that is not yours to bear.

Just what do people bring to your life? What do they expose you to? Some people want to expose you to ideas, philosophies and anything else they have been exposed to. Some people want to expose you to things that are not good because some of your "friends" (even some relatives and friends) want to make you into someone they are comfortable with. Some people will use what you are uncomfortable with to make you *more* uncomfortable. A smoker will expose you to smoking, a "user" will encourage you to use people and a manipulator will encourage you to find your way into people's lives to make them do what you want them to do.

Be careful of who enters your life. There are a people who come into your life to wreak havoc and destruction. However, if your heart is centered "in" Jesus, you will not be led astray. You have the gift of discernment and will recognize what the enemy is trying to steal from you. The devil is always recruiting new vessels. Who you call your "friends" and who you admire speak volumes about you. Some people want to bring things to your life you have no use for. There is a case for "attracting who you are". Kindred spirits attract each other. Some people that have nothing in common with you may be attracted to you. There are a couple of reasons for it; one is some people may see something in you that they want to possess. This may include the fact that some people may see your "demeanor", not quite realizing what it is but wanting to learn more about it.

This is where the Lord gives you an opportunity to show the curious or interested person the ways of Jesus. People observe you whether you realize it or not. We understand that some unbelievers may have no use for the Lord. These people come to harass you or anyone else that walk in God's light. There are people, however, that are truly seeking something beyond themselves. Maybe they have never seen an example of anyone in "the light" until they met you. Sometimes people see you *evolve* into a person that walks the "narrow path".

Another type of person, someone that is not a kindred spirit is someone that comes to make you into someone they are comfortable with. These can be people that newly infiltrate your life or people you may have known for a long time. Regardless, they enter your life in order to introduce traits, habits and vices into your life that as a man or woman of God, you have no use for. These people are attracted to you because you are polar opposites of them. It will be noted here that not everyone who have certain vices will attempt to get you to experiment with them. There are people you know that respect your choices; as a matter of fact, since they know that you are a non-participant of any vice they participate in, they will *discourage* you from doing so.

The issue here are people that want to encourage you to participate in habits that would go against God's standards. Some of these types of people are in bondage and they want you to join them. They do not like that idea that you seem to be free from addictions. You are the "anti them". If you are a non-drinker, there may be someone you know that will encourage/insist, that you take a drink. One of the manifestations of a man or woman of God is humility. A "braggart" will arrive to "toot his own horn" as he hates humility because his puppet master, the devil, hates humility too. Whatever characteristics the devil has, his vessels will possess also; after-all, *they are a reflection of him.*

Since a manifestation of demonic activity is chaos, the "enemy" will insure that he brings confusion and strife to any atmosphere where God's peace is in place. The "atmosphere" can be an area such as your home, place of employment, church or the peace may be imbedded in your heart. Where ever the peace is, the devil will come in an attempt to replace it with his influence. Keep in mind that any attack can come from an acquaintance or stranger as any other attack can but the intent here is to have you to be aware of the devil's wiles because many times he operates from "within".

The world does not set standards for us; God does. There is never any need to walk in any paths that God has not set us on. There are people who think they are in a position to decide who you should be. There is no need for anyone to be present in our lives who cannot encourage us to be all we can be in the Lord. There are enough challenges in our lives *when we are alone* to deal with without having negative influences in other people who want to send us in the wrong direction. Unless someone can encourage us to make right decisions we should probably keep our distance. The Lord understands that there are not perfect people but there is no need to fall further away from His will. The fact that "no one is perfect" is not an excuse not to try to be the best we can be. "Enter through the narrow gate. For wide is the gate and broad is the road that leads to destruction, and many enter through it", Matthew 7:13, NIV.

Your Ministry

You have a ministry. Your ministry is wherever God has placed you and people can see *Him* in you. Your place of employment can be your ministry or your home. You can have multiple ministries in as many places (territories) as God has given you. It is God's will that you reach as many of His people as possible and also people who want to receive the priceless salvation offered by Jesus Christ. People are looking for answers. They are looking to come to grips with a past that they connect to carnally but not spiritually. In other words, they have not spiritually discerned incidents from their past and the connections the past has concerning them in the present. God can use you to point struggling people *forward*.

We have all been through *something*. The devil plotted to have early traumas destroy us. God's purpose was to use the work of the devil to strengthen us for His Glory. The Lord used evil for our betterment. There was never a times when God did not keep His hand on us. We are still here. They enemy did not mean for us to survive his snares. He did not mean for us to still be here. Satan meant for us to lose our minds, lose our ways and turn our backs on God. Since his previous attempts did not "take us out" he will continually come up with new ways to side-track us. The enemy will also continue to try old tricks he may have been successful with in the past.

God's will is for us to recognize a demonic attack when it appears. If a vessel of the "enemy" informs you that you will fail a class and you were originally told that lie earlier in your life, a proper Spiritual response would be, "oh, that's just the devil again" and then *ignore that lie.* If you had never known adversity, you never would have been given "territory" nor would you have a ministry because you would not know anything. If you had never had a trial, you would not be able to over-come adversity because you would not be strong enough to do so. If you had never been though a "test" you would not understand *grace* since grace is an attribute of God. He states that "My Grace is sufficient for you, for my power is made perfect in weakness", 2 Corinthians 12:9, NIV. With the power of His Father on His side, Jesus could have had a luxurious lifestyle. He chose a life that would benefit us. He certainly did not endure hardships because He enjoyed it. He *suffered* trials. The trials, persecutions and crucifixion were pre-ordained by His Father and sent Jesus into His destiny. Joseph was sold into slavery by his brothers, Genesis 37:28, and became the governor of Egypt, Genesis 41:46 NIV. Trials and tests lead and connect you to your destiny. Peaks and valleys are part of our journey.

It is unrealistic not expect trials. It is the devil that sought and continues to seek our destruction. It is Satan that wants us to remain in bondage and hold the Lord and other people responsible for our trials. The devil uses trials to distract us and the Lord uses trials to teach, minister, correct and show His power. The Lord wastes nothing. Everything is used for His purpose. When the devil unleashes an attack on you whether through your mind, his vessels or other circumstances, he surely does not have any good in mind for you. There are no good lessons from the devil; Jesus said "The thief comes *only* to steal and kill and destroy, John 10:10, NIV. Also in John 10:10, Jesus goes on to say, "I have come that they may have life, and have it to the full", NIV. Use your trials and tests to gain wisdom from the Lord to dispense that wisdom for the good of His kingdom.

Shift Change

Change is vital; it is necessary for growth. It is essential for promotion. It is part of the journey that God uses to get us where He needs us to be. It is also important because God gave us a spirit of adventure and curiosity. The Lord gave us a spirit of exploration and He expects us to use it. There are "pulls and pushes" in life that lead us from one point to another. Life is a series of mysteries. Sometimes when we have plans in our lives, an unexpected event can cause plans to go awry. There has never been a human in the history of mankind that could say that they have had a dull life.

There are certain events in our lives that cause us to flow in another direction. God keeps things interesting. He deliberately directs us into "spheres". "If the Lord delights in a man's way, he makes his steps firm", Psalms 37:23, NIV. There are no accidents. Every move or shift is calculated by the Lord. They are designed to bring us to places physically and more importantly, spiritually, that God uses to bring us into fullness in Him. God allows change to ensure that we will meet new people, see new places, find adventure and gain new insight. Life is a series of updates. Information that once "worked" in our lives may not be what "works" later with the updated information we gained.

There are many God ordained changes we make. "God ordained" is used here to denote the fact that when we feel as if *we* are making a change, it was *God's* prompting that moved us to make that choice. That means that the move or decision was Spiritual and was made from your heart, not your mind. You followed the prompting of the Holy Spirit. If the "move" was made in the context of a career move, the motivation may have been a promotion; either in finances, position *or* the move may have been made for relocation purposes. Maybe the move may have been a combination of all three. Regardless, it was not as much as your decision as you thought it was.

A job or career change goes beyond "change". It represents a *shift* in your life. It is a shift because God caused it. It is also a "shift" because typically it is a Spiritual promotion. A Spiritual promotion is parallel with a promotion that brings you into a higher level in God. Much like carnal education, once you have completed a grade, you are ready for the next level. Changing jobs goes beyond bettering yourself financially or by position. It brings you into contact with new "teachers" because God will bring you to new possibilities with new people, some of whom have *ministries*. God brings you into contact with other people because He has given them information that He wants you to have. There are people that can give you ministering or advice that can assist in you in your purpose in life.

The conclusion of anything can represent a shift in your life. The end of a relationship is a "shift change". Depending on the circumstances, the ending of a relationship may signal the beginning of newness. Usually, at least one person involved in the relationship is disappointed /hurt at the ending of a relationship. Regardless, if you are the one that has been disappointed you will find yourself in a new sphere. New because, you will no longer be around the friends of the person you were in a relationship with. You will be meeting new people and going new places even if you do not engage into another relationship anytime soon after the one that ended. It is a new adventure. The ending of something is always the beginning of something new.

There will be times when other people will "move" or make changes in their lives that will bring them into proximity to you. It is not an accident that the new employee's cubicle is next to yours. *You* can represent a shift for someone or people in general. Just your influence or *call* from the Lord can bring a shift in someone's spiritual outlook and therefore a promotion. Everyone you meet is a chance for growth. A verbal exchange with a stranger in a grocery store is not benign. *It is an exchange of concepts and ideas between two spiritual beings even if the subject was the weather forecast.*

Don't underestimate your travels in life. Try shopping at different stores or take a different route to work. Have a conversation with the person you have never had one with at work. Naturally, you cannot interact with everyone. Too many people are vessels for the enemy and are more than willing to ensnare you at the enemy's behest because he comes as an "angel of light". "For such men are false apostles, deceitful workmen, masquerading as apostles of Christ", 2 Corinthians 11:13, NIV.

Allow God to take you places spiritually and physically. He gave us a spirit of adventure. Each person we meet is an opportunity for growth. Don't dismiss a possible acquaintance because you cannot discern something carnal or tangible that you can benefit from. Too many men and women are notorious for not becoming acquainted with members of the opposite sex because they are not "dateable". It is unfortunate that many of us will not become involved with other people unless there is something to gain such as money, sex, a "shoulder to cry on", status or someone that will "do things for me". There are an untold amount of blessings that people have missed out on because they "dismissed" people that were deemed not "datable".

God places ministering spirits in many people "Be not forgetful to entertain strangers, for by so doing some people have entertained angels without knowing it", Hebrews 13:2, NIV. Shifts in your life can take in many forms. Anytime you take on a new endeavor, there will be a "shift". Starting a business or enrolling in school are two examples of shift changes. The devil's desire is that we are stagnant; not moving, doubting God's promises. The enemy also desires that we do not satisfy the gifts of discovery or adventure. The less we experience and learn the more the enemy can keep us in bondage. He knows the consequences of not experiencing God's desires for us, "My people are destroyed from lack of knowledge", Hosea 4:6, NIV.

Don't allow yourself to miss out of the adventures God has set out for you. There is much to discover in life. There are people that get into comfort zones and are fearful on unknown. There are "roads" the Lord has mapped out for all of us. The "enemy" will see to it that his vessels and his insidious influence follow you to new horizons. The devil will never cease in his pursuit in sending his demon spirits to distract you when you have "shifts" in your life. He never gives up. Just remember that the Lord will be with you where He places you.

There are times when doubt may set in when we make a decision in our lives. This is natural because there is a tendency to questions ourselves when we make a big move especially if there is a "setback" when doing so. All doubts and fears come from the enemy. Since it is not the devil that set us upon a new endeavor, there is no need to listen to him when he plants negative thoughts in our minds. The Lord sets His plans in motion for our lives and He will give us everything we need to succeed.

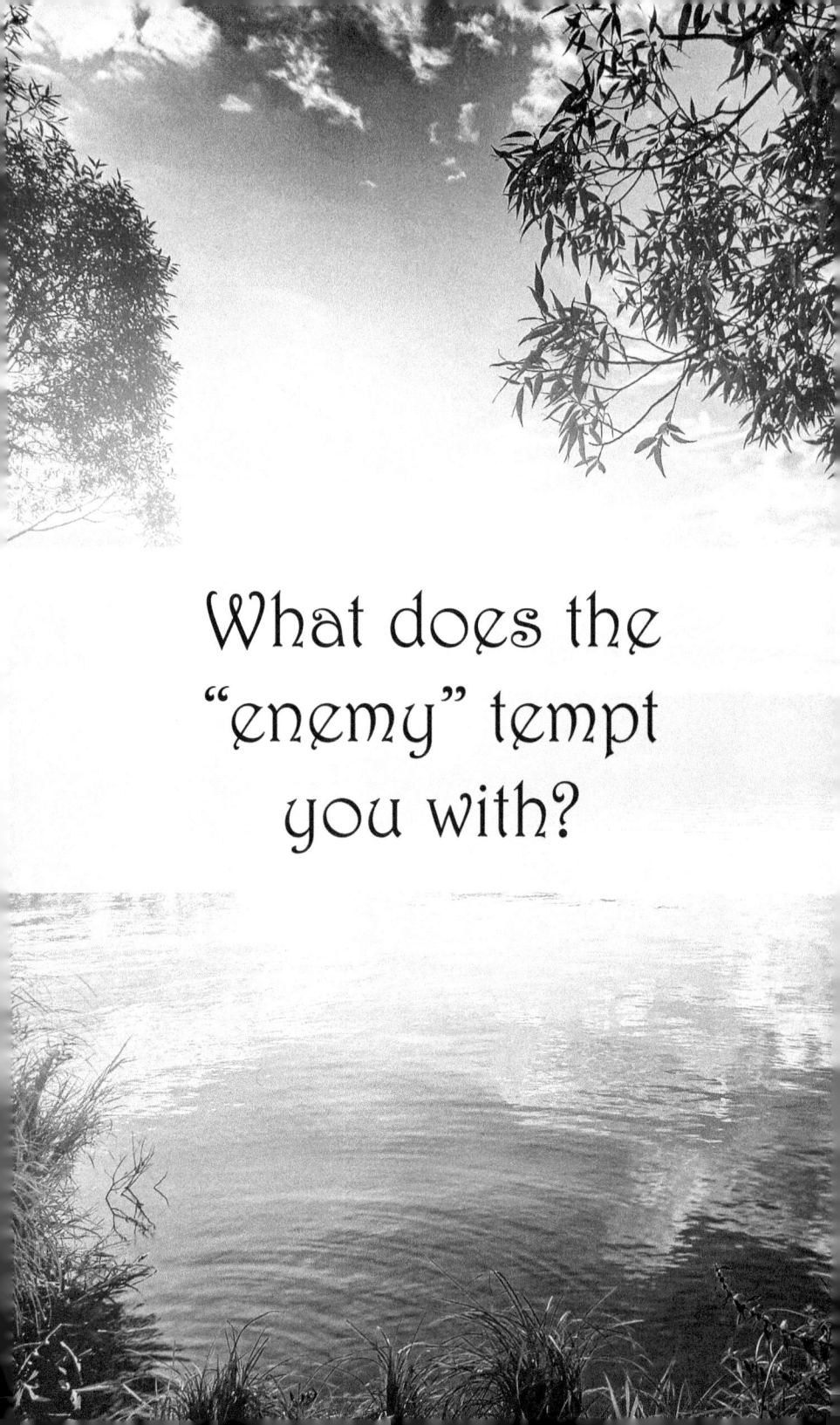

What does the
"enemy" tempt
you with?

The saying goes "everybody has a price". Is this a human philosophy or a *demonic* truth? God does not tempt anyone and gives us a way out of temptation. "No temptation has overtaken you except what is common to mankind. And God is faithful; he will not let you be tempted beyond what you can bear. But when you are tempted, he will also provide a way out so that you can endure it", 1 Corinthians 10:13, NIV. The devil's mantra is "I know what you like and you cannot resist it".

Due to the fact that the devil has scouted us, he does know what we like. He knows how to dress it up, how to package it, where to place it and how *much* of it to place. He knows *when* to put it there too. The "tempter" creates the perfect storm to entrap us. The "who, what, where, why and how" all intersect at the enemy's behest to create a breeding ground to make us fall. The devil uses temptations to distract and to dishonor ourselves. He uses temptation to condemn us if we fall into his traps. The enemy tempts, persuades and condemns.

The more "avenues" or vulnerabilities to certain sins, the more the devil has to lure us away with. Whatever the devil can tempt us with has to be acknowledged and be given over to God. Jesus states in John 14:30 that "I will not say much more to you, for the prince of this world is coming. He has no hold over me", NIV. This is the will of God; that the devil has *no hold over any of us* and that he has nothing he can accuse us of and nothing to tempt us with. Satan's name means accuser and he will do what he names suggests whether there has been a sin committed or not. If we never sinned he would *accuse* us of trying to be perfect.

In fact, in his double talk, the devil will use the mantra "nobody's perfect" in justifying sin. He will then *accuse and condemn* you after the deed is done. In our humanity, we use the "nobody's perfect" mantra when we go amiss. Be assured that God does not adhere to this principle. The Lord is not a god of excuses. He knows that through Him, we can overcome temptation, *any* temptation.

The devil will tempt you according to your spiritual authority. The smaller your spiritual authority or "sphere" of influence, the less he needs to lure you with. It does not take much for him to tempt the "simple" minded (he may not even bother with them) but he offers an infinite amount of bait to you if you have a large amount of spiritual authority; the larger your "sphere" the more the bait. The devil offered (tempted) Jesus Christ influence of all the kingdoms of the world if He, Jesus, would worship him. "Again, the devil took him to a very high mountain and showed him *all* the kingdoms of the world and their splendor", (italics mine) Matthew, 4:8, NIV. Since Jesus came to offer salvation and save the world, which represented a threat to the devil's influence in the world, the devil tried to buy him off to keep Him *away* from His destiny, salvation for the world.

The devil does not waste any time in tempting people who have no influence. That may be because in many cases, these types of people do not pose a threat to his kingdom *or* he did tempt such people and they "bought". Again, it does not take much for the devil to tempt the "simpleton" because he poses absolutely no threat. A "simpleton" flows along the path the enemy lays out for him and is satisfied with the smallest things (crumbs) the enemy offers him and blows up or exaggerates the importance of those crumbs in his mind and to other people. *He serves only himself.* This is to the devil's delight.

It may not be in the same setting as the top of a mountain where the devil encountered Jesus when he showed him the kingdoms of the world but the temptation from the devil will come to you as it always has. The devil can come to you in a dream or he can come to you in a thought. He can send people or one person to tempt you. The term "tempt" is not used here in conjunction with the temptation of the occasional sin (although *any* sin is against the will of God), it is used in conjunction with the *total* turning over of a person's life to the devil's "promises" that keep that person from serving God's kingdom. Many people have prospered financially because they took on a life (crime for just one example) that the devil tempted them with.

The enemy "tempts" to distract you and to *keep you away from your destiny that the Lord has set out for you; the bigger the blessings God has planned for you, the bigger the offer from the enemy.* We are on this Earth to serve on behalf of God. We are not here to compromise that service. Temptation serves itself; it is the absolute opposite of service and is rooted in selfishness. God has a purpose for us all.

Be careful of any offers that sound too good to be true. Put God first and ask Him to guide you through decisions. Since the devil comes as "an angel of light"("And now wonder, for Satan himself masquerades as an angel of light", 2 Corinthians 11:14, NIV) he can be very crafty and convince you that an incredible offer is from God. The enemy is a master deceiver. This is where your gift of discernment will assist you. Stand on the promises of God. Nothing Satan can offer us can match the plans God has for our lives. "For I know the plans I have for you", declares the Lord, "plans to prosper you and not harm you, plans to give you hope and a future", Jeremiah 29:11, NIV.

Satan's plans are to give *himself* hope and a future at your expense. His doom is certain and his will is to take you and as many others to the same fate. Matthew 6:24 states, "No one can serve two masters. Either you will hate the one and love the other, or you will be devoted to the one and despise the other. You cannot serve both", NIV. As far as God is concerned this scripture is an un-compromised fact. As far as the devil is concerned, *he is willing to compromise*. He wants you to "serve two masters" because he knows that if you are attempting to serve him *and* God, you are compromising your relationship with God and he, the devil, can gain a foothold into your life. Keep in mind that the devil would love your total devotion but he is willing to "take what he can get" and work from that.

There is no amount of money or whatever the devil offers that can minutely compare to the life that God have planned for you. Watch out for friends, family or strangers who approach you with ideas that do not come from God. People who care about you will never involve you into something that goes against your beliefs but there may be someone placed close to you by the devil who will attempt to lure you into a "deal" with the enemy. Be aware that Satan tempts us with wrong desires every day. There is no such thing as "small sins" in God's Holiness. The issue here is making sure that the very life God gave you is not manifested in such a way that would glorify the devil. He has nothing worthy to offer. All that we need in this life are the blessings of God. Do not allow peer pressure (demonic vessels) to lead you into forfeiting your Spiritual authority. Life has so much to offer. God has a plan for you. Too many people feel as if "service" means *sub*-servient, (*beneath*) and in their pride, refuse to be of service to anyone. They are here to serve themselves, *only*.

God, the Director

There are no accidents; everywhere you go is an opportunity to meet other people; Spirits. Where God directs your steps, you will bless someone. Where we direct our own steps, selfishness ensues. Some people would be surprised if they knew the lives they touched if they knew the effects of a pleasant greeting. It may mean a lot more to someone who is having a "bad day" than they realize. "The steps of a *good* man are ordered by the Lord; and he delights in his way", Psalm 37:23, King James Bible. *The Lord directed you to assist that person with car trouble.*

Throughout your life, there will be incidences that you may overlook and not realize that the Lord directed you to where and when you appeared on His behalf. At times it will seem as if you happened to "come across" someone in need. Of course, you cannot help everybody. Some people who will refuse your help do not need it. Throughout the Bible are instances where God directed someone to assist, bless or teach people in general along their paths or they were sent directly to a place to a specific person.

It is God's will that you spread as much of His influence as possible. He wants His holiness seen in you. Many people want to see an example of God in you even if they are unbelievers. We live in a world where mankind is not always so "kind". When God directs your steps to assist or bless someone, He is sending you to someone that needs what you bring through Him. Someone needs to hear what you have to say. God understands that some people are vexing. It takes a lot of energy to deal with such people even if you are well meaning. These people *cannot* accept goodness from you or anyone else.

Sometimes it will be people that are familiar with you who will reject what you have to offer even if it is from the Lord. Something you have to offer may be rejected because *it is* from the Lord. Offering an assist to some people who cannot receive it is akin to "casting pearls to swine", "Give not that which is holy unto the dogs, neither cast ye pearls before swine, or they will trample them under their feet, and turn again and rend you", Matthew, 7:6, King James Bible.

Jesus did not go where he was not wanted and He does not expect you to do so either. God will assign you territory in which to perform His will. He will give you the Spiritual authority to assist and bless. Your place of work is a prime place for such territory because your job is more than a place where you earn you living; *it also your ministry. Any* place you spend as much time as your place of work, home, church, half-way house, women /homeless shelters or any other place where the wisdom of God is needed is your ministry.

Where ever your ministry is (your territory) there will be negative influences. There will be the devil's vessels in the same areas to negate God's "light". The devil does not want the wisdom of God in places he wants to occupy. His vessels are there to harass you. These people have nothing to offer; they just want to keeps you from your assignment. They will keep wary eyes on you and "report back" to someone they feel have more physical/carnal authority.

The problem with this is that the authority figure's incentive is apt to be rooted in pride and ego and has nothing to do with the will of God; he is not there to help, he is there to hinder. The territory you are assigned to is yours. When you operate outside the territory God of that has assigned you, you miss, the assignment. But the *assigned* territory is another matter because not only does the Lord direct your steps to people He has assigned you to, *He will send people into your assigned territory to accomplish the same will.* God will direct other people and send them into your territory.

In the context of anywhere else God has assigned you, there will be efforts to displace you. God will not allow anyone to stop what He has already prophesized will happen. The main thing is standing in faith that the Lord will give you the strength to withstand the wiles of the enemy. One thing Satan counts on is people who are working for God to leave the area he or she is assigned to. We should never run from persecution unless and until God has decided that you are needed in another place in order for His influence to take root there. Be advised that God will provide periods of rest, yet you may be sent into hostile territory. *God's peace and will shall win-out.*

You assignment in this world was pre-determined by God. He left no stone unturned. You are kindred spirits with Mordecai, Mary, Samson, David, Esther, Naomi and Abraham just to name a few. These brave men and women are only a *few* prime examples the Lord wants us to emulate. Some of them did deeds that angered God but we all have. In fact, they are an example that God uses people to bring about His will regardless of their backgrounds. Never feel that God cannot use you. God gives us all we need when He directs our steps. Wherever He needs us, he provides wisdom first. He gives us resources and sends us a helper/mentor. The Lord gives us information as needed so do not expect all the answers at once. Go where God sends you; you will be a blessing to someone.

Rejection, Acceptance and the five senses

The "five senses" of taste, touch, smell, hearing and sight. We know how vital they are. They serve us well physically. They do not serve us well spiritually. In fact, the five senses can be a detriment in our lives when used incorrectly. Taste can identify what we want to eat or dislike, touch can identify something too hot to feel, smell identifies an aroma we like or identifies smoke to alert us to danger. Hearing can also act as an alarm by way of a motorist blowing his car horn to warn us. Sight is used for physically visualizing the world.

When it comes to a "spiritual vision" or discernment, the five senses are not what we should rely on because they give us the wrong information. When it comes to dealing with life, God gave us Himself to gain information. The Lord's information is never wrong. It is information that can carry us because He knows and sees all things. Information that is not available to us in the physical realm is readily available in the spiritual realm. That is where we should look.

A case will be made here that although the five senses do serve us well in the physical sense, they can make a world of difference *spiritually*. Hearing and sight can be used for the things of God. Jesus *implores* us to "listen if you have ears". Then Jesus said, "Whoever has ears to hear, let them hear", Mark, 4:9, NIV. Jesus is referring to spiritual hearing; *listening with your heart*. There is *spiritual* sight; seeing life or situations through *in*sight or discernment by seeing things through God's eyes and wisdom. Spiritual ears and eyes have a place in our lives when used correctly and directed by God.

Insight is the order of the day when it comes to discernment. Some of life's "issues" can be solved or at the very least, insight can be gained into situations that are important. Many people have issues with rejection. We are human and sometimes there are no words that can soothe us when we feel as if someone thinks we do not "measure up" This is a lie from the devil.

"Rejection" in the physical realm is a lie. In other words, rejection does not mean you do not "measure up". That is the lie the enemy wants you to believe. Rejection is confusing in the physical sense because it causes us to questions ourselves. Being accepted tends to give us comfort because by feeling accepted, *questions have been answered.* It is within our human nature to desire acceptance. We arrived in this world feeling accepted due to being in our mother's womb and the subsequent welcoming we received when we were born.

Unfortunately, sometime later in life, we find that we will not always be welcomed. There will be people and circumstances that would rather go in another direction rather than be with us. A potential employer will hire someone else other than us. Someone we think we would like to enter a relationship with may have other plans that do not include us. If we use the gift of discernment, including our spiritual ears and eyes, we can see that the "denial" of a job or someone we like will work *for* us, not against us. God equipped us with *Him*. Through God we will see that people and things we think are so important are not as important as we think. This is not to trivialize any person. It just means that through God, we realize that it is not in our best interest to pursue certain matters any further.

In the context of inter-personal relationships, if you are the recipient of "rejection" remember, it is *not* personal. If just feels that way. There are times when we should place ourselves in the shoes of the person we feel has rejected us and try to see things the way they do. Realize that their goal is not to make you feel rejected. Their goal is to be happy, same as yours. Their happiness is not dependent on us being in their lives just as our happiness is not dependent on them being in our lives.

In essence, rejection is not personal. It is the denial of an entrance of a person into someone's life. Defined another way; it is *you* denying someone an entrance into *your* life. People who are "rejected" also reject other people. When we meet someone we like, the five senses, (physically) take over. That is, we use the sense of sight, (physical attraction). After meeting and the subsequent conversation, we like the way the person sounds (hearing). Perhaps the person has a nice fragrance using a quality cologne or perfume, (smell). After a gentle caress (touch) we would like to "pursue things further".

Physically, two people can be attracted to each other. *But* if one or both people have a God-centered spirit heart, what does *it* say? Two people can be compatible in almost every facet but the relationship can be overruled by *one* God-centered heart. Just because two people are compatible on many levels does not mean that they are compatible spiritually. Here is where the conflict lies. When two people meet for the first time, they may not know each other psychologically but they know each other spiritually. God *connected* people spiritually but not psychologically. He is a Spirit and is connected to us. He did not place us among each other for *dis*-connection. If the Lord had placed us in this life and not connected us in spirit, we would not know our potential mate when the Lord brought us face to face with that person, (more about that later). The individual spirits of everyone operate and communicate independently of our physical interactions. In the context of a potential relationship, while we are in courtship phase, another interaction is going on in the spiritual realm between two people. Remember, the spirits of two people have to have common ground (kindred spirits). Terms such as "spirit self", "higher self" or "God-centered" heart will be used in regard to the following scenarios.

The God-centered heart (spirit) of "Carol" may not feel kindred with the spirit of her suitor, "Mike", even though she likes him physically and emotionally. If not, her God-centered heart will let her mind know that spiritually, it does not want to be involved with the *spirit* of "Mike". If her mind listens to her heart (her *spiritual* ears) she will "back away" from the relationship with "Mike". *Understand that the decision to back away from the relationship is coming from God via her heart and not the "physical" Carol.* There *can* be a relationship if two people are not kindred spirits but whether it can be a *good* relationship is another matter.

Sometimes when we make a decision, one way or another, we may not realize mentally that the decision came from our God-centered heart. We think we made the decision from our own "wisdom" There is a disconnection when we don't realize that any wise decision we make came from God. There are times when our pride tells us that we deserve all the credit and we assign the credit to ourselves. God has guided us when we did not know He was at work in our lives. Gratitude is due the Lord. He is our protector.

Getting back to "Carol", she now has to inform "Mike" that she cannot have a relationship with him. He, of course, is disappointed and wonders if he did anything wrong. This is the first sign that he is taking the so-called "rejection" personally. We know that "Carol's" decision to end the relationship came from her God-centered heart which makes the rejection *spiritual in its' nature and not personal.* "Mike" is agitated but after attempting to reconcile with Carol and being denied any further dalliances in her life, decides to "move on".

Here is another example using the same scenario; "Carol's" God- centered heart does not feel kindred with "Mike's" spirit. In this scenario, she ignores what God is telling her in her heart. She has decided that she wants to enter a relationship with him regardless of the "nagging feeling" in her mind (she has not discerned that the "nagging feeling" is her higher spiritual-self telling her it does not want to be in relationship with the higher spirit-self of Mike), does not want to be in a relationship with him, Mike.

Carol may be ignoring those "nagging feelings" but Mike is beginning to feel strange about being in a relationship with her. He cannot quite "put his finger" on it but *something* seems amiss. He calls Carol and tells her that he thinks it would be better if they decided to not take things any further. She, of course, is surprised. *What just happened here?*. Carol may have ignored what her spirit-self attempted to tell her but the message came across to the spirit of Mike's loud and clear. It was stated earlier that Carol's spirit-self did not feel kindred with the spirit of Mike's and communicated the information to "it".

Mike's spirit-self received the information. In turn it was communicated to his mind. Though he could not quite "put his finger" on what "nagging feeling" was, there was something in his spirit that told him he was not welcomed in Carol's life. He ended the relationship and in this scenario, Carol felt rejected, although it was her spirit self that rejected Mike *first*. All Mike did was leave the relationship based on the information *he received from Carol's Spirit.*

The God-centered heart or higher-self is the protector in all of us because it is where our Lord dwells. So- called rejection can come prior to or the early onset of a relationship. It can become a factor after a relationship has gone on for an extended period of time. God can and will give us discernment to understand "rejection" but our ego must be put away. This is because ego, pride and bitterness will block any understanding. It was stated earlier that God made us for spiritual connection. This does not mean that we can be kindred spirits with everyone. It means that the Lord wants us spiritually connected for reason of compassion and God views us as His family. Spiritual connection serves this purpose because it allows us to share in joy and pain. It also makes us aware spiritually, what to discern in each other. We cannot read minds but with the gift of discernment, we can "search hearts". Spiritual connection can show who is for us or against us. It is not to be used for judgment but can be used to correct our brother in Jesus' name. It is also used by God to show who belongs in your life and who does not. If you are single and hoping to be married, spiritual connection can lead you to the person God has for you because you will recognize this person when you meet him or her. Your *spirit* or higher-self will reveal your future spouse if you are tuned into God. He is your "center" and He dwells in your spirit-self.

If you are a man, the beauty you see in the woman God has for you will have physical beauty but the very essence of her beauty will be spiritual. God will see to it that you notice her beautiful spirit before you notice her physical beauty. In simpler times and before egotism became so prevalent, inner beauty was held in high esteem. The Lord meant for men to "find" a wife, *not look for her*. "He who *finds* a wife finds what is good and receives favor from the Lord", Proverbs, 18:22, NIV.

According to Proverbs, 18:22, a woman is to be *found* by the man God has planned for her. God "directs the steps of a good man" therefore a good man will be *directed* to find her. God will place her in a "good man's" path. Some people and especially women, tend to see relationships that do not work as "failed relationships". There are no failed relationships, only learning experiences. Furthermore, if a woman has a God-centered heart, that heart will "dismiss" anyone that is not kindred in nature. The spirit-filled or God-centered heart will *continue* to dismiss potential mates until it meets someone with a spirit that connects and is kindred to hers. Her God-centered heart will recognize the spirit-self of that man *before* she recognizes the physical attributes of him.

"Rejection" has a negative connotation because of the human definition. *Vocabulary.com* defines "rejection" as a noun and to the "actual act of rejecting something or to the *feeling* one has after being *rejected.* In other words, you might have *feelings* of rejection after experiencing the rejection of others", (italics theirs). Rejection is a *feeling.* Feelings are not based on reality. They are based on perception. The only perception that counts is God's. The Lord is the "reality". What does He tell you when things do not go according to *your* plans? Understand that God blocks relationships and uses divine intervention.

The Lord, through spiritual discernment, tells us what He feels. Rejection to us is acceptance in Him. The perception we have about someone is often at odds with who they are spiritually, (we often judge a book by its cover).God knows the full spiritual DNA of everyone that has ever been born and those of people who *will* be born. We may feel rejected when we are denied an employment opportunity. Spiritually, if you are denied an employment opportunity, it may be because the Lord has another opportunity for you. You are working for His glory, not for yourself. There are of reasons that God may not want you in a certain "sphere" or territory. One reason is that the Lord may have enough of His people in that territory and His influence may be better served another area. If you are denied an opportunity it goes beyond the people that did not hire you. Look for other opportunities to serve the Lord where ever He places you. God is the ultimate career counselor. We have to look beyond ourselves. The feeling of rejection is rooted in *the flesh not getting what it wants.*

Pride

Dictionary.com defines 1"pride" as "a high or inordinate opinion of one's own dignity, importance, merit, or superiority, whether as cherished in the mind or as displayed in bearing and conduct". 2 The state or feeling of being proud". The Bible states that "Pride goes before destruction, a haughty spirit before a fall", Proverbs, 16:18, NIV. The catch phrase in the first definition from *Dictionary.com* is "cherished in the mind". A heart that lack humility allows the mind to magnify and exaggerate traits that do not come from God. A heart of humility can receive God's light without pride. Pride and God cannot co-exist in the heart.

Pride is an exaggerated sense of one's self-importance. It is self-serving and demand's its' own exaltation. The people who live through pride seem to glow in their arrogance. Arrogance is the cousin of pride. "Pride" can have a positive connotation; you can take pride in your work or become *prideful* when you feel as if you have done a good job. The former comes from God and the latter is physical. The devil understands the snares of pride because it was his pride that got him kicked out of heaven. Lucifer had angels that told him that he was as important as the Lord and that he could replace God. A person full of pride will also have followers that will encourage his prideful behavior. After Lucifer was ejected from heaven, the angels who encouraged him were also ejected.

You will notice that people who are prideful have many admirers. These people (admirers) are for the ego gratification of the prideful person and are parallel to people who are the "narcissistic supply" to the narcissist. People who are "know-it-alls" have behavior rooted in pride. They do not listen to other opinions or feedback. They don't even listen to God. Many mistakes are documented in the Bible due to pride. King Nebuchadnezzar's pride (book of Daniel) convinced him that Shadrach, Meshach and Abednego (Daniel 3:20,NIV) should worship the idols he had set up. When someone is operating out of pride, all spiritual awareness and logic is cast aside. It is an evil spell as is all spirits that operate outside the will of God. There is a conflict with a prideful person and one with a heart of humility. This is because pride is an attribute of the devil and humility is an attribute of the

Lord. Spiritual warfare will ensue because pride *must control its environment.* Since the world views kindness or humility as weakness, the person operating in pride will attempt to control and dominate anyone with a heart for the Lord.

Anyone in the vicinity of the prideful person and identifies with such a spirit, will be recruited into the will of that person. It is also a main ingredient for a cult; a prideful, charismatic person luring people into his group by way of pride that is manifested through personality. The cult will have spiritual philosophies and doctrines that do not come in agreement with the will of God. Pride is dangerous. It is not to be taken lightly since *all sin is rooted in pride* and "self". The "look at me" mantra by prideful people does not serve God's kingdom. The only way pride can be ejected from the heart is thorough a cleansing by God. Only God can renew our minds and spirits but we have to welcome Him into our hearts.

"Living the Bible"

"If the world hates you, keep in mind that it hated me first", John 15:19, NIV. Jesus was hated. His followers were hated then and they are hated now. People are known to hate entire families; they usually do not hate *one* family member. If you are a member of Jesus' family, you will be hated also. There are sacrifices that have to be made if you belong to the Lord's family. You will not have many friends. You will have many enemies. The persecution you suffer will be because you have chosen to server your "Holy Teacher" instead of people.

In our humanity (relying too much on our physical senses), we often miss a picture that goes beyond what we see with our physical eyes. Adverse human behavior against us is usually analyzed in the realm of psychology. We tend to view a situation that was based in the spiritual realm and see it in the personal or carnal realm. Persecution is not a physical concept. It is spiritually based. The mind is too complicated to figure out. There is a reason psychologists educate themselves for years learning the nuances of the mind. There is a concept called "simple mindedness" but *the mind is not simple.*

Most of us do not have the gift of understanding the mind in the same manner that psychologists do. We must use discernment. Discernment is the wisdom of God and does not takes years of education to learn it. This is certainly not an indictment of the hard work put in by doctors who have studied the mind. They are, after all, gifted in areas of understanding that the Lord has called them to do.

Nothing in our lives that has occurred is new because history repeats itself. We are all similar to the people who wrote the Bible and the people the Bible speaks of. There is a "David" in many men who become enamored by a woman as David did with Bathsheba and who then proceeded to have an adulterous relationship with that woman. Maybe the woman's husband was not set up for death as Bathsheba's husband was by David (2 Samuel, 11:15, NIV) but perhaps the "killing" came at the expense of other people by way of divorce or other "emotional injuries".

There is a "Samson" in many men; men who trusted the wrong woman. There have been men who trusted a woman who was looking for an area of weakness in him in order to "bring him down" and destroy him (Judges 16:5, NIV). Delilah led Samson to his demise but Samson bears major responsibility because he trusted someone that *was not trustworthy* (in the final analysis, we are all own worst enemy). The spirit of "Paul" exists in many people. Paul was originally a murderer of Christians (Acts 7:60, NIV). Paul, however, was delivered from his hatred of God's people and became a prophet *for* God and preached the Good News. (Acts 9:4, NIV). God can convert anyone He chooses.

David was also a king and led the nation of Israel. God can use us in spite of our faults and short-comings. Samson, in his death, killed more of God's enemies, the Philistines, than he did in his life, Judges 16:30, NIV. A spirit of jealousy lives in the lives in many of us because of someone's popularity, deeds, reputation or a combination of all three. Jealousy is a dangerous trait and is rooted in insecurity. Saul was determined to kill David because David became popular, 1 Samuel 19:1, NIV. Saul's *perception* was that David was a threat. *Saul lost his throne because of his disobedience to God, not because of David,* 1 Samuel 15:23, NIV. Could jealousy be a major cause of murder today? The first murder in world history was caused by jealousy; Cain killed his brother, Abel, Genesis 4:8, NIV. Perhaps a precedent was set for jealousy as a major motive for murder.

Since evil spirits are not taken to the grave, they must find new vessels. They may roam the Earth for a short while but they invariably find other "homes" to reside in. Jezebel became queen of Israel when her husband, Ahab, became king, 1 Kings 16:29, NIV. She hated God and His prophets and was killed by Jehu but her spirit lives on. You can see this insidious spirit throughout society. Hopefully, while still mortal in our bodies, all adverse spirits will be ejected from our hearts prior to "passing on".

There is a perverse air of manipulation in the world today. Control, bitterness and total hatred of God and His people are common place. These are only a few of the manifestations of the Jezebel spirit. The Book of Esther shows that Esther was an example of God anointing someone to save her people from elimination. Esther was also an example of God ordaining someone to take on tasks that are above us yet within us for God's purpose. She went to the king at the risk of death when she approached King Xerxes to tell him that Haman, who hated the Jews and wanted to have them slaughtered, Esther, 5:2, NIV. The Lord is currently in the process of raising His people to stand up for His kingdom.

We are currently *living* the Bible. If the world hated Jesus, it will hate you also. In turn if someone slams the door in your face, they have slammed the door in God's face. If someone insults you, they have insulted God since you belong to Him. It is the same if you have children; if someone harms your child, they have disrespected you since that child is *connected* to you.

The husband that throws a punch at his wife has thrown a punch at Jesus. Husbands are to love their wives as God loves the church, Ephesians, 5:25, NIV. The husband that harms his wife disrespects God also. Many people commit acts of sin and think there are no spiritual repercussions. They falsely believe that if they do not answer to a physical source such as the judicial system, they have gotten away with the deed. Sin always goes further than immediate repercussions. The husband that harms his wife has no idea that what he is also doing is sinning against God. He thinks that the police are the *only* people he has to deal with when he commits acts of aggression against his wife.

You can read your Bible and see that there are many people that God would want us to emulate. The Lord ultimately wants us to emulate His only begotten Son, Jesus Christ. There were many evil people in the Bible whose evil spirits live among us today. There were also many brave men and women that worked for the Lord. The spirits of them live in many men and women today. There are people, who prior to a revelation with, God, sought their own way; their own path. Esther was originally fearful to approach King Xerxes because a person could not approach the king unless that person was summoned. Esther found a cause that was *higher than her.* This is the understanding that God wants us to believe in; that in any cause that is in His name, He will anoint you for that assignment. As in any anointing, "self" cannot be prevalent.